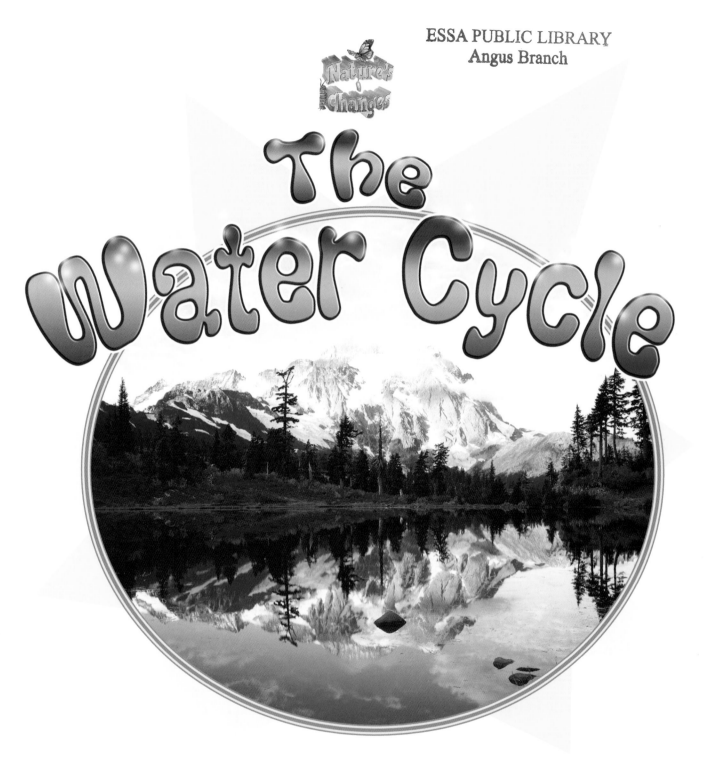

The Water Cycle

Nature's Changes

Bobbie Kalman & Rebecca Sjonger

Crabtree Publishing Company

www.crabtreebooks.com

Created by Bobbie Kalman

Dedicated by Heather Fitzpatrick
To my dear friend Marcelle Welch, who honors all the Earth's elements

Editor-in-Chief
Bobbie Kalman

Writing team
Bobbie Kalman
Rebecca Sjonger

Editors
Molly Aloian
Robin Johnson
Kelley MacAulay
Kathryn Smithyman

Design
Margaret Amy Salter

Production coordinator
Heather Fitzpatrick

Photo research
Crystal Foxton

Consultant
Dr. Richard Cheel, Professor of Earth Sciences, Brock University

Special thanks to
Sophie Izikson

Illustrations
Barbara Bedell: pages 9, 10
Katherine Kantor: page 12
Robert MacGregor: page 19
Margaret Amy Salter: page 20

Photographs
BigStockPhoto.com: Eli Mordechai: page 18; Jason Stitt: page 23 (top)
iStockphoto.com: Paige Falk: page 16; Michael Karlsson: page 25 (top);
    David Maczkowiack: page 25 (bottom); Kokleong Tan: page 23 (bottom)
Bobbie Kalman: page 31 (top)
Other images by Adobe Image Library, Comstock, Corbis, Corel,
    Digital Stock, Digital Vision, Ingram Photo Objects, MetaPhotos,
    Photodisc, TongRo Image Stock, and Weatherstock

Crabtree Publishing Company

www.crabtreebooks.com   1-800-387-7650

Cataloging-in-Publication Data
Kalman, Bobbie.
  The water cycle / Bobbie Kalman & Rebecca Sjonger.
     p. cm. -- (Nature's changes)
  Includes index.
  ISBN-13: 978-0-7787-2276-2 (rlb)
  ISBN-10: 0-7787-2276-7 (rlb)
  ISBN-13: 978-0-7787-2310-3 (pbk)
  ISBN-10: 0-7787-2310-0 (pbk)
  1. Water--Juvenile literature. 2. Hydrologic cycle--Juvenile literature.
I. Sjonger, Rebecca. II. Title. III. Series.
  GB662.3.K354 2006
  551.48--dc22

**Published in
the United States**
PMB 16A
350 Fifth Ave.
Suite 3308
New York, NY
10118

**Published
in Canada**
616 Welland Ave.
St. Catharines, Ontario
L2M 5V6

**Published in the
United Kingdom**
White Cross Mills
High Town, Lancaster
LA1 4XS

**Published
in Australia**
386 Mt. Alexander Rd.
Ascot Vale (Melbourne)
VIC 3032

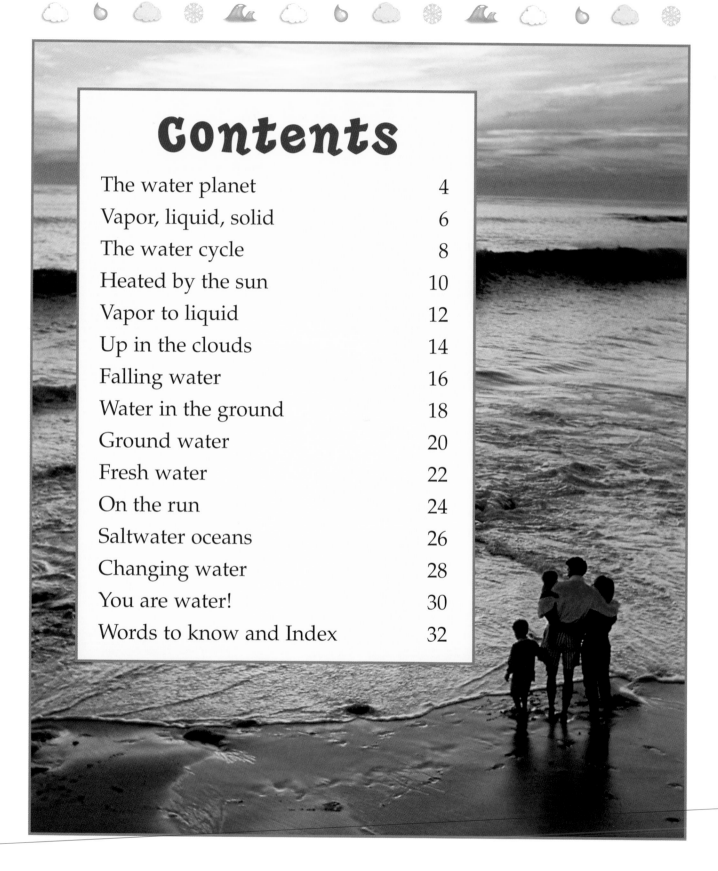

Contents

The water planet

Look at all the blue parts on Earth. They are water. Earth is sometimes called "the water planet" because it has so much water. Almost all the water on Earth is in oceans. There is also water in lakes, ponds, rivers, and streams. There is even water under the ground!

We need water!

Without water, there would be no living things on Earth. All living things need water to survive. Plants cannot grow without water. Animals and people cannot live very long without water, either.

Animals and people need to drink water to stay alive. These zebras are having a drink on a hot day.

Plants need water to stay alive. The roots of these new plants take in water from the ground.

vapor, liquid, solid

Water is always changing. It changes when it is heated. It also changes when it is cooled. **Water vapor**, **liquid**, and **solid** are the three forms of water. Water vapor is a gas. When water is a liquid, you can drink it. You can also swim in it. Solid water is snow or ice.

From liquid to vapor

When water is heated, it changes to water vapor. You can see water vapor coming off water boiling in a kettle. On a cold day, your breath also contains water vapor.

Snow and ice are solid water.

From vapor to liquid

Water vapor returns to liquid when the air around it cools. If you hold a cold glass near the steam from a kettle, drops of water will form on the glass.

Liquid and solid

Liquid water becomes solid when it freezes. When snow or ice melts, it becomes liquid again.

The water cycle

Water moves as it changes form. It moves from the ground up into the sky as water vapor. It then falls back down to Earth as rain or snow. The movement of water into the air and back to Earth is called the **water cycle**.

Around and around

The sun and wind move water. Water becomes part of the clouds, part of the ground, part of plants, animals, and people, and part of the oceans. Oceans contain **water currents**, which also move water from place to place.

It never stops!

The water cycle never stops. Water does not stay in one place. It moves from one part of the world to another. The next page shows the changes in the water cycle.

Water words

The words in this box help explain how water changes form in the water cycle.

condensation Condensation takes place when water vapor meets cold air and changes into liquid.

evaporation When water is heated and changes from liquid water to water vapor, evaporation takes place.

ground water Water that is under the ground is called ground water.

precipitation Water that falls from the sky is called precipitation. Rain, snow, **hail**, and **sleet** are kinds of precipitation.

transpiration Plants **absorb**, or take in, water from soil. Transpiration takes place when plants let off water vapor through their leaves.

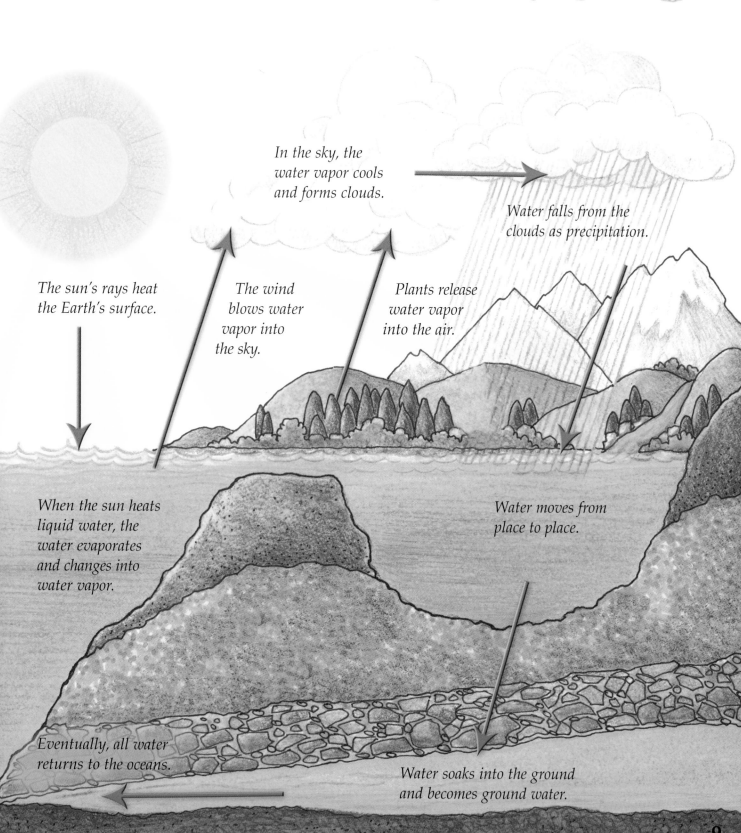

In the sky, the water vapor cools and forms clouds.

Water falls from the clouds as precipitation.

The sun's rays heat the Earth's surface.

The wind blows water vapor into the sky.

Plants release water vapor into the air.

When the sun heats liquid water, the water evaporates and changes into water vapor.

Water moves from place to place.

Eventually, all water returns to the oceans.

Water soaks into the ground and becomes ground water.

Heated by the sun

The sun heats water.

When water is heated, it evaporates.

Heat from the sun warms Earth and everything on it. The **surface**, or top layer, of water in oceans, rivers, and lakes warms the most. Water evaporates from the surface and becomes water vapor. On a hot day, a lot of water warms up. Evaporation happens quickly in hot weather. In cool weather, evaporation takes place slowly.

Evaporation happens quickly on a hot sunny day!

Into the air

Water vapor is in the air all around you, even when you cannot see it! On a hot day, the air may feel **humid**, or damp. Humid air contains a lot of water vapor. The wind lifts some water vapor high into the sky. It may also blow water vapor far from the place where it was liquid water.

*Sometimes you can see water vapor in the air. It is called **mist**.*

vapor to liquid

2. *High in the sky, the air is cold. Water vapor condenses and forms tiny drops of water.*

1. *The sun heats the air near Earth. Hot air rises up into the sky.*

The wind carries water vapor high into the sky, where the air is colder. When the water vapor becomes colder, it changes from a gas into tiny drops of water. Changing from a gas to a liquid is called condensation. Condensation often happens high in the sky because cold air cannot hold as much water vapor as warm air can.

Try it yourself

You can watch condensation happen. Pour very cold water into a glass. Wait for a few minutes, watching the glass closely. You will see drops of water form on the outside of the glass. Where did they come from? They came from the air around you. When water vapor in the air met with the cold glass, drops of water formed on the glass.

Morning dew

Without the sun's heat, air is colder at night than it is during the day. Water vapor condenses in the cold night air and covers Earth with **dew**. Dew is drops of water that form on cool surfaces during the night. The temperature at which dew forms is called the **dew point**.

You can see drops of dew on this leaf. The tiny tree frog will drink some of the water. Other animals also drink dew.

up in the clouds

When tiny water drops bump into
one another in the sky, they form large
drops. Thousands of large drops may
join together. When they do, they form
clouds. Clouds can be many shapes
and sizes. The way a cloud looks
depends on the temperature of the
air, the direction of the wind, and
how high the cloud is in the sky.

14

Which cloud is which?

People can **predict**, or guess, what the weather will be like by looking at the clouds. White, wispy clouds are called **cirrus clouds**. Cirrus clouds form high in the sky and usually mean there is little chance of rain. Big, puffy clouds are called **cumulus clouds**. Cumulus clouds often form in the sky before thunderstorms.

These thin clouds are cirrus clouds.

Cumulus clouds usually have flat bottoms and fluffy-looking tops.

***Fog** is cloud that forms close to the ground.*

Falling water

Clouds that contain many water droplets may create precipitation. Precipitation falls to the ground as rain, snow, hail, or sleet. Rain may fall to the ground in a light sprinkle or a heavy **downpour**. Snow may fall as a few flakes or a big snowstorm. Hail is made up of balls of ice called hailstones. Hailstones can be as big as baseballs! Sleet is precipitation that is a mixture of rain, snow, and hail.

How precipitation forms

Clouds that form low in the sky are made up of water drops. Rain may form in these clouds. It takes hundreds of water drops to make a single drop of rain! When clouds form very high in the sky, they are made up mainly of **ice crystals**. When many ice crystals join together, they form a snowflake. The heavy snowflakes fall to the ground as snow.

Oceans and mountains

Areas of land that are near oceans receive much more precipitation than do areas that are far from oceans. Areas near mountains, as shown below, also receive a lot of precipitation. When clouds rise to pass over mountains, they hit cold air. They cannot hold their water vapor in cold air. Rain or snow then falls from the clouds.

Water in the ground

Some precipitation that falls on land soaks into the soil. Water that stays in the soil near the surface of the ground is called **soil moisture**. Plant roots absorb soil moisture. The plants use the water to grow.

Dry soil absorbs more water than does soil that is already wet. If the soil is already wet, puddles form on the surface of the ground. Animals drink water from the puddles.

These arrows show water evaporating from the leaves.

stem

soil

water

roots

Transpiration

Water may remain as soil moisture for a short time or a long time. Some soil moisture is absorbed by plants. As plants make food, they release water through their leaves. The water evaporates and becomes part of the water cycle again. Evaporation through plant leaves is called transpiration.

Releasing water

A plant pulls water up through its roots and stem and into its leaves. The leaves have tiny holes called **stomata**. Some water leaves the plant through the stomata. Once it is outside the plant, the water evaporates.

Ground water

Some water in the soil trickles deep into the ground. This water is called ground water. Eventually, ground water collects in **aquifers**. Aquifers are layers of rocks that are deep under the soil in the **saturated zone** (see page 21). Aquifers have tiny holes in them, so they can absorb and hold water. Eventually, the ground water seeps out of the aquifers. It flows into rivers and streams.

The water in this stream was once in underground aquifers.

The unsaturated zone

There are spaces in the soil near the surface of the ground. The spaces in the soil are filled with soil moisture or air. There is always some air in the soil, so it is not **saturated**, or soaked with water. The layer of soil that contains both soil moisture and air is called the **unsaturated zone**.

The saturated zone

Some water flows deeper into the ground and becomes ground water. This water collects among soil and rocks. At a certain point, so much water collects that the soil becomes completely saturated with water. This layer of the ground is called the saturated zone. In the saturated zone, soil contains no air.

soil

rocks

unsaturated zone

saturated zone

Water and air fill the spaces between the soil and rocks in the unsaturated zone. In the saturated zone, ground water fills all the spaces between the soil and rocks.

Fresh water

Ground water and the water in lakes and streams is **fresh water**. Fresh water does not contain a lot of salt, so it is safe to drink. Many living things need fresh water to survive. Fresh water is not just found in liquid form. More than two-thirds of Earth's fresh water is in the form of ice and snow!

Collecting water

People use fresh water for drinking, cooking, taking baths, and washing clothes. To make sure there is enough water for everyone to use, people collect and store fresh water. They store it in large tanks or **reservoirs**. A reservoir, shown below, is a human-made lake.

On the run

Not all precipitation soaks into the ground. In some places, the ground is too steeply sloped or too rocky to absorb water. Saturated soil also cannot absorb water. Some rain and melting snow trickles downhill over land. Water that trickles over land is called **runoff**. Runoff flows into lakes, rivers, and streams. Runoff eventually ends up back in oceans, just as all water does.

Runoff in cities

There is a lot of runoff in towns and cities because water cannot soak through pavement. Most of the runoff flows into **sewers**. Sewers are underground pipes that carry runoff to rivers, lakes, and oceans. Some sewers carry waste, as well.

*Without sewers, runoff might **flood** city streets.*

This ground cannot absorb any more water. The water that is not absorbed will become runoff.

Saltwater oceans

All runoff contains tiny bits of rocks and **minerals**. Salt is one of the minerals it contains, so runoff is slightly salty. Water has been moving through the water cycle for millions of years! For all that time, runoff has been carrying salty water to the oceans. That is why oceans contain **salt water**.

Ocean animals

Millions of animals live in oceans. Their bodies are perfectly suited to living in salt water. In fact, if there was no salt water, ocean animals would die!

Changing water

The water on Earth today is the same water that was here long ago! The water is changing, however. Much of it is being **polluted**, or made unclean, by the actions of people. Cars and factories produce poisonous **chemicals** and gases. Some of these harmful poisons soak into soil and pollute the ground water. Other chemicals become part of the air. When it rains or snows, chemicals mix with the water and create **acid rain**. Acid rain is precipitation that contains poisonous chemicals. It harms plants and animals and pollutes water in oceans, rivers, lakes, and streams.

Warming oceans

Some scientists believe that pollution causes Earth to become warmer each year. Warmer temperatures on Earth then cause the oceans to become warmer. Warmer oceans lead to changes in the weather. They create more rain and may also cause huge storms called **hurricanes**. Hurricanes are fast-moving wind storms that form over oceans. When the winds blow over land, they lift ocean water onto land.

Even small changes in the temperature of oceans can cause ocean plants and animals to die.

On land, hurricanes cause a lot of damage!

You are water!

Earth is different from other planets because it contains water. Water is everywhere, and it is in everything. Plants and animals are made mostly of water. Rocks are shaped by water. The soil holds water.

Water moves

Water runs in rivers,
crashes as mighty waves,
falls as gentle rain,
cascades as waterfalls,
drifts as delicate snowflakes,
rolls as blankets of fog,
and always returns to
the oceans.

We love water!

When we look into the sky,
We can see water in the clouds.
Sometimes it falls on our faces as rain;
sometimes as snow.
We love water in all its different forms.
We love to drink it, hot or cold.
We love to bathe and swim in it.
We love to ski over snowy hills
and skate on slippery ice.
When the sun shines through water in the air,
the water shows the colors of sunlight,
and a beautiful rainbow appears.
We especially love rainbows!

We need water!

Most of Earth is made up of water.
Most of our bodies are made of water, too.
We are watery creatures,
living on a watery planet.
Without water, our bodies could not work.
Our blood could not carry
oxygen to our lungs.
Our brains could not think.
Our bones would break.
We could not eat.
Every part of our bodies needs water!

Water keeps us alive!

Sometimes we forget
how important water is to us.
We waste it or make it dirty.
We think we have more than enough,
but there is not much clean water left.
We need to respect water.
We need to be thankful for water.
We need to love water.
We need to remember that
water keeps us alive!

You are water!

To show how you feel about
water, say these words:
"I love you water."
"I thank you water."
"I respect you water."
And—don't forget, YOU ARE WATER!

Words to know

Note: Boldfaced words that are defined in the text may not appear on this page.

chemical A natural or human-made substance that can be harmful to living things

downpour A heavy rainfall

flood To overflow with large amounts of water

hail Balls of ice that fall from certain clouds

humid Describing air that contains a lot of water vapor

ice crystal A small piece of ice that forms in the sky when the air is cold

liquid A form of water that flows freely

mineral A crystal in the soil that helps plants grow

salt water Water that contains a lot of salt

sleet Hail that is mixed with rain or snow

solid A form of water that has a firm shape

water current A strong movement of water in a certain direction

Index

1 2 3 4 5 6 7 8 9 0 Printed in the U.S.A. 5 4 3 2 1 0 9 8 7 6